RECOGNIZING HIS VOICE
IN A WORLD FULL OF NOISE

HEARING
GOD

Unless otherwise noted, all Scripture references are taken from The Holy Bible, New International Version®, NIV®. Copyright ©1973, 1978, 1984, 2011 by Biblica, Inc.™ Used by permission of Zondervan. All rights reserved worldwide. www.zondervan.com The "NIV" and "New International Version" are trademarks registered in the United States Patent and Trademark Office by Biblica, Inc.™

Scripture quotations marked (NLT) are taken from the Holy Bible, New Living Translation, copyright © 1996, 2004, 2007, 2013 by Tyndale House Foundation. Used by permission of Tyndale House Publishers, Inc., Carol Stream, Illinois 60188. All rights reserved.

www.milestonechurch.com

ISBN: 978-1-954961-16-6
Printed in the United States.

RECOGNIZING HIS VOICE
IN A WORLD FULL OF NOISE

HEARING
GOD

HERE'S THE PLAN

1

Grow closer to God as you understand and study His Word.

2

Study the introduction individually.

Study Weeks 1-6 with a group.

3

Discover how to hear God's voice through the different ways He speaks to us.

HOW THIS GUIDE WORKS

READ THE CHAPTER

Concept

Context

Passage

What Does
This Mean for Us?

What Do I
Do with This?

INTERACT WITH THE CONCEPTS

Take notes
in the margins.

Write out answers
to the questions.

Memorize the verse
and think about the
key truth each week.

(Cards located in the back
of this guide.)

TALK ABOUT IT WITH YOUR GROUP

Starting
with
Week One:

"God
Speaks through
His Word"

TABLE OF CONTENTS

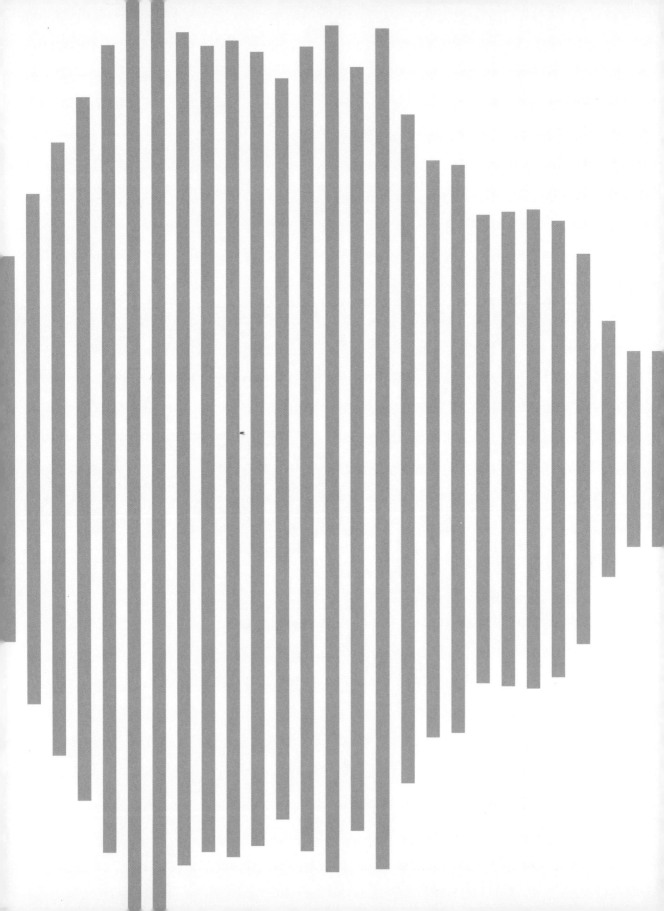

GOD SPEAKS– HE'S A COMMUNICATOR

CONCEPT

We can say a lot with only a few simple words.

Have you ever heard someone say, "God spoke to me"? Maybe you've even said it yourself.

It's quite the statement.

You're telling me the uncreated, eternal, holy Creator of the heavens and the earth looked in your direction and gave you a specific message He wanted you to know?

It's a big deal.

Most of us don't know how to feel about it. This makes sense. When we consider this idea, we're filled with all kinds of questions.

- What did He say?
- How can you tell?
- What did He sound like?
- How do you know it was Him?
- Were you prepared for this kind of moment?

And perhaps most importantly … **what are you going to do about it?**

Why is God speaking to me?

When God has words, we have questions.

When God speaks, we think: *Why is God speaking to me? He must be looking for someone else. I'm not the right person.*

If you've ever felt this way, you're in good company. Some of the most well-known characters in the Bible felt this way.

- When God spoke to Abraham and told him he would have a son, Abraham said it was impossible. (GENESIS 17:17)
- When God told Abraham's 90-year-old barren wife the same message, she laughed.[1]
- When God met Moses in a burning bush and told him to go free His people from Egypt, Moses told God He picked the wrong guy. (EXODUS 3:11)
- When God came to a man hiding in fear and called him a "mighty warrior," Gideon said he was the smallest guy in the weakest family.[2]
- When King David was old and reflecting on everything God had done for him, he could not understand why God would speak to him, love him, and pour out His goodness throughout his whole life. (1 CHRONICLES 29:14)

These were ordinary people with big problems. None of them were expecting a divine encounter with God where He would speak directly to them.

> **Genesis 17:17**
>
> Abraham fell face-down; he laughed and said to himself, "Will a son be born to a man a hundred years old? Will Sarah bear a child at the age of ninety?"

> **Exodus 3:11**
>
> But Moses said to God, "Who am I that I should go to Pharaoh and bring the Israelites out of Egypt?"

> **1 Chronicles 29:14**
>
> "But who am I, and who are my people, that we should be able to give as generously as this? Everything comes from you, and we have given you only what comes from your hand."

---

1 Sarah was eavesdropping when God spoke to Abraham and she laughed. Later God asked her about it and she was afraid so she lied. God wasn't offended. He loved her anyway. And when the baby did come, she named him Isaac, which means "he laughs."

2 On this list, Gideon is one of the lesser-known characters. You can read the whole story in Judges 6-8.

We don't expect it either. He doesn't come on our schedule. If we knew God was coming with a message for us, we would probably cancel everything on the calendar so we could be ready and waiting.

Or maybe we would get scared because of the pressure. It feels like a lot.

But this is who God is. It's who He's always been.

God is a communicator. He's always speaking and His words carry unimaginable power.

He spoke the world into existence. When He said, "Let there be light," galaxies were illuminated. Because He never said, "Stop!" the universe continues to expand at the speed of light.

From the very beginning, God has been speaking to His people on a daily basis with the intended purpose of developing and strengthening their relationship while providing regular guidance and encouragement.

Look at the first chapter of the first book of the Bible. As soon as He made people in His image, He started speaking to them. He blesses them and tells them to be fruitful, to fill the earth, and to take good care of it (GENESIS 1:27-29).

Genesis 1:27-29

[27] So God created mankind in his own image, in the image of God he created them; male and female he created them. [28] God blessed them and said to them, "Be fruitful and increase in number; fill the earth and subdue it. Rule over the fish in the sea and the birds in the sky and over every living creature that moves on the ground." [29] Then God said, "I give you every seed-bearing plant on the face of the whole earth and every tree that has fruit with seed in it. They will be yours for food."

This is how God set up the world. He hasn't changed His mind. He still wants it to work this way.

God would come to visit His family in the Garden of Eden in the cool of the day to walk and talk with them. This was their regular routine (GENESIS 3:8a).

Now it may not seem like a big deal, but this detail is really important. Most people think God only cares or thinks about super-spiritual things like worship services and the deep realities of the universe, or that He's busy with holy rituals.

But these ideas do not come from the Bible.

In God's Word, from the outset, God showed up where His people were. He went to their home, which was also their office. He walked and talked with them about what was happening in their lives. It was ordinary. It was relational. It was normal. He was interested and had things to say about what they were doing.

He still is and He still does. He cares about you.

The question is not, would God swing by your spot in the cool of the day to speak with you? The question is, when He does, are you listening?

There's one more detail from the story we need to consider.

Genesis 3:8a

Then the man and his wife heard the sound of the Lord God as he was walking in the garden in the cool of the day ...

Genesis 3:1 tells us about an adversary who inserts himself into the conversation. The first thing he does is question what God said in order to foster uncertainty and doubt regarding God's intentions toward His people.

Since then, there has been a spy, an enemy who has committed all of his resources to interfere, sabotage, and disrupt the dialogue.

It makes so much sense.

Why is it hard to hear God? Because we don't know how it works. We don't know what He sounds like. We don't know how He feels about us. We think He's busy and interested in other things.

And there's an enemy trying to sabotage our communication.

No wonder this is difficult.

And we haven't even mentioned the fact we all bring our own baggage to the conversation. There are all kinds of issues that make this hard. Because we're anxious, stressed, and overscheduled, we have a hard time paying attention. Because we carry guilt and shame for the mistakes we've made, we don't think God wants to speak to us. Because our world is cynical and pessimistic, it's easier for us to doubt what we hear than to believe it's God.

Genesis 3:1

Now the serpent was more crafty than any of the wild animals the Lord God had made. He said to the woman, "Did God really say, 'You must not eat from any tree in the garden'?"

In addition, most of the time when we think about hearing God, we're looking for direction for our future. This creates significant pressure.

- What if I misheard what He said?
- What if I make the wrong choice?
- If I choose option A when God wanted me to choose B, will I mess up the rest of my life?
- If I make that mistake, will God ever trust me enough to speak to me again?

If you can relate to any of these scenarios, you know how difficult and complicated this can be.

This is why God wants to make it simple to learn to hear from Him. And it's available to anyone who will receive the gift.

We learn to hear God through the person of Jesus.

The Gospel of John was written by one of Jesus' closest friends. He opens the book with this profound statement: "In the beginning was the Word, and the Word was with God, and the Word was God" (JOHN 1:1).

What does this mean? You cannot separate God from His Word. They are the same.

And then John hits us with a massive plot twist in John 1:14: "The Word became flesh and made his dwelling among us. We have seen his glory, the glory of the one and only Son, who came from the Father, full of grace and truth."

Jesus, God's one and only Son, the Living Word, who is God and has been with God from the very beginning, moved into our neighborhood to show us what God is like.

This is the story of the New Testament and the entire Bible. Hebrews 1:3 says Jesus is the exact representation of God. Colossians 1:15 tells us the Son is the image of the invisible God.

Jesus shows us who God is. Jesus shows us how to hear God. And Jesus gives us His promise, His guarantee we can do it.

Hebrews 1:3

The Son is the radiance of God's glory and the exact representation of his being, sustaining all things by his powerful word. After he had provided purification for sins, he sat down at the right hand of the Majesty in heaven.

Colossians 1:15

The Son is the image of the invisible God, the firstborn over all creation.

CONTEXT

In Jesus' day, many of the people could not see He was the Son of God, the Living Word. They did not believe Jesus was the way we hear God.

In John 9, Jesus heals a man who was born blind. As you might imagine, it creates a big commotion. The Pharisees (religious scholars/political leaders) were troubled by it and investigated the man and his parents.

The Pharisees cared about their traditions, their beliefs, and their cultural influence. Jesus cared about the man. This escalated the tension between them, and so in response, Jesus gave a lengthy teaching about sheep and shepherds.

When Jesus calls Himself the Good Shepherd, the Pharisees would have immediately thought of two significant passages of Scripture.

 In Psalm 23:1, David famously writes, "The Lord is my shepherd, I lack nothing." During his days as a shepherd, the Holy Spirit

Psalm 23:1-4

[1] The Lord is my shepherd, I lack nothing. [2] He makes me lie down in green pastures, he leads me beside quiet waters, [3] he refreshes my soul. He guides me along the right paths for his name's sake. [4] Even though I walk through the darkest valley, I will fear no evil, for you are with me; your rod and your staff, they comfort me.

inspired David to see God as our Shepherd. We are His sheep. We are dependent on Him. He cares for us, provides for us, protects us, and guides us. His goodness and mercy will follow us all of our days and we will be with Him forever.

Jesus is saying, "That's who I am."

The less familiar passage is a contrast by warning. Ezekiel 34 describes the anger the Lord has toward evil shepherds who treat the people harshly and care only for themselves. Because of their wickedness, God comes to care for the sheep Himself.

Jesus is not-so-subtly telling the Pharisees, "That's who you are."

Jesus makes His statements about who He is and what He's come to do in the middle of this very contentious conversation.

Ezekiel 34:10-11

[10] "This is what the Sovereign Lord says: I am against the shepherds and will hold them accountable for my flock. I will remove them from tending the flock so that the shepherds can no longer feed themselves. I will rescue my flock from their mouths, and it will no longer be food for them. [11] For this is what the Sovereign Lord says: I myself will search for my sheep and look after them."

I am the good shepherd.

JOHN 10:2-3, 11, 14-15, 27 (NIV)

2 "The one who enters by the gate is the shepherd of the sheep. 3 The gatekeeper opens the gate for him, and the sheep listen to his voice. He calls his own sheep by name and leads them out."

---

11 "I am the good shepherd. The good shepherd lays down his life for the sheep."

---

14 "I am the good shepherd; I know my sheep and my sheep know me—15 just as the Father knows me and I know the Father—and I lay down my life for the sheep."

---

27 "My sheep listen to my voice; I know them, and they follow me."

. . . they follow me . . .

WHAT DOES THIS MEAN FOR US?

In this passage, Jesus repeats Himself for emphasis and makes an incredible promise.

He is the Good Shepherd and His followers are His sheep. He calls them by name, He leads them out, and they know His voice.

Think about that. One of the greatest fears we have is to be unseen and unknown. We worry, *Does God know what I'm going through? Does He see me? Has He forgotten about me?* Jesus reminds us that He sees us, He knows us, He calls us by name, and He leads us out.

He's got a plan. He's preparing for our future. He knows what we don't know.

He is the Good Shepherd because He lays down His life for the sheep. He is the Good Shepherd because He knows His sheep in the same way as He knows the Father.

Without any qualifiers or conditions, Jesus promises: **My sheep listen to (hear) My voice.**

What does it take to hear God? Do you have to be special? Does it require perfect obedience? Do you have to memorize the Bible? Do you need secret knowledge of deep spiritual truths?

That's what the Pharisees believed—and many people believe it today.

Not Jesus. The only thing you need is to be His sheep.

The reason this is so significant is it takes away all the things outside of our control. We don't have to be anxious or stressed. He put the pressure on Himself. He's a Good Shepherd.

JESUS SPEAKS TO US, PROVIDES FOR US, GUIDES US, AND DIRECTS US.

We just need to listen.

Let the reality of this push back against the anxiety or worry you may feel in this area. The problem is not whether God will speak to us. Jesus has settled that question.

The question is, **will we listen when He speaks?**

WHAT DO I DO WITH THIS?

First, you've got to decide whether or not you're one of His sheep.

Sheep are not the smartest animals. They scare easily. They have to be led gently. They are keenly aware of the other sheep. They can't be treated harshly. They are dependent on the guidance of the shepherd.

Does this sound like your relationship with God? Or do you tend to be more self-reliant?

Is your first thought, *I've got this* or, *My situation is unique?* Do you keep Jesus sequestered to one part of your life and only go to Him in case of an emergency?

Many of us don't intend to live this way but it's often where we end up. This may explain why you're struggling to hear Him.

Hearing God begins with recognizing and admitting how much you need His voice.

 Second, you prioritize His voice above the others. In John 10:5, Jesus says the sheep don't follow the voice of a stranger. Instead, they run from those voices because they don't recognize them.

We've never had more strangers telling us how to live our lives.

Jesus says the people who genuinely follow Him can tell the difference between His voice and everyone else. Sheep aren't perfect. They don't always get it right . . . especially when they're stressed and afraid. But once they see the shepherd, they follow. We would be wise to do the same.

> ### John 10:5
>
> "But they will never follow a stranger; in fact, they will run away from him because they do not recognize a stranger's voice."

GOD SPEAKS, SO WE NEED TO LISTEN.

JOHN 10:27 (NIV)

"My sheep listen
to my voice;
I know them, and
they follow me."

MEMORY VERSE

Use this space to write down
the memory verse. If you do
this multiple times each week,
it will help you memorize it.

*"My sheep listen to my voice;
I know them, and they follow me."*

John 10:27

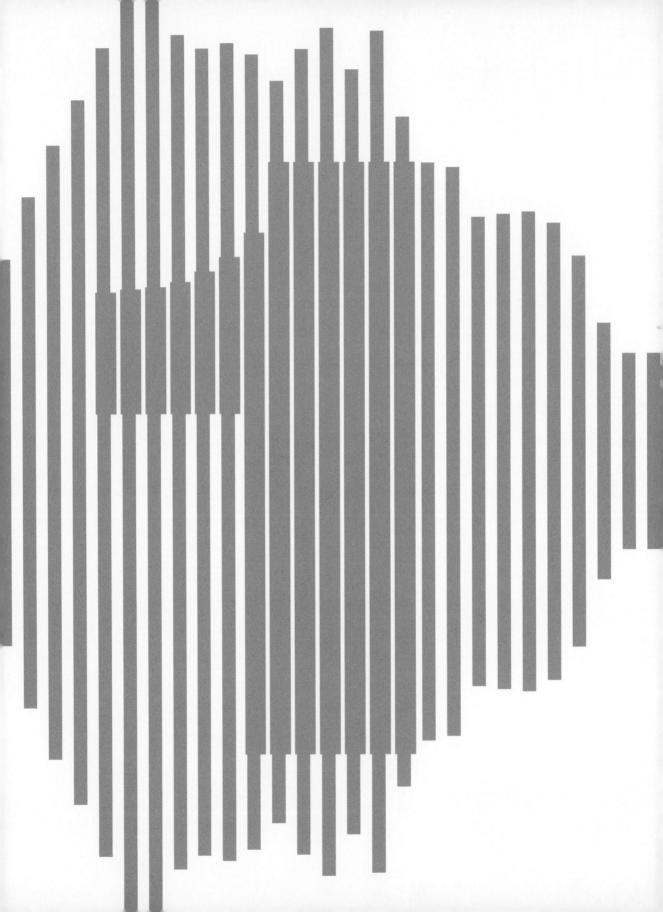

WEEK ONE

GOD SPEAKS THROUGH HIS WORD

CONCEPT

It's one of the most common questions followers of Jesus wrestle with:

WHAT IS GOD SAYING TO ME?

If only we knew. If only we could be certain and confident. And perhaps most importantly, can anyone help us understand how it works?

Learning to hear God's voice works like learning to hear anyone else's voice—just like parents and children, co-workers, or close friends. You recognize it after you regularly hear it. And the best place to regularly hear God's voice is through His Word, the Bible.

Because it's so large and filled with different types of writing, it can be easy to treat the Bible like a Magic 8 Ball or a collection of random, potentially meaningful statements like the message in a fortune cookie.

What is God Saying to me?

At other times, the Bible feels a world away—like it has nothing to do with where we live.

How do we make sense of it? Where do we start? Because sooner or later, we all come to moments where we need help and guidance from someone who knows what we don't.

We have more information available to us than ever before. With a few swipes and clicks, we can search just about anything. With Google, Wikipedia, and WebMD, we feel like we can figure most things out.

These things can be helpful, but most of the time, they can't tell us what's really going on inside of us.

Proverbs 20:5 says the purposes of a person's heart are deep waters, but one with understanding draws them out.

That kind of understanding doesn't come from a search engine or swiping on social media.

It has been said there are only three kinds of information in life: the things we know, the things we don't know, and the things *we don't know* we don't know.

At key moments in our lives, we're searching for the answers to deeply personal questions.

Have you ever thought:
- How did I get to this point in my life?
- Why did it happen this way? Is it too late for me to change?
- What does God want from me? How do I know?
- What am I supposed to do next?

When someone suggests God is present and active in our lives and willing to speak to these issues, it leads to a new set of questions:
- Does God provide these kinds of answers?
- If so, what do you have to do in order to find out?
- How does His Word help us know?

The first and most important change we have to make is to understand that God wants us to approach His Word to have a relationship *with* Him more than to get information *from* Him.

CONTEXT

Samuel is one of the most important and trustworthy people in the Old Testament. God gives him the responsibility of hearing and representing His Word as He allows the people to establish a kingship in Israel.

This bothered Samuel because he believed God was their King. But the people wanted a king like everyone else. You follow and obey the king, and the desires and needs of the king become a big influence in your life. Samuel knew God's desire was to make them a special people close to Him. A king would be a distraction from the voice of God.

But when Samuel prayed about it, the Lord told him to go ahead because they were rejecting God, not Samuel.

All of the drama around choosing a king happened near the end of his life, but this story gives us a window into how Samuel learned to hear the voice of God as a boy. While Samuel's ability to hear and obey God's voice was a unique gift, his story provides

1 Samuel 8:7

And the Lord told him: "Listen to all that the people are saying to you; it is not you they have rejected, but they have rejected me as their king."

insights into God's character and nature all of us can learn from.

A woman named Hannah was deeply saddened because she could have no children. She prayed and told the Lord that if He would give her a son, she would dedicate him to the Lord. She prayed with so much passion that Eli the priest thought she was drunk. She told him she hadn't been drinking; she had poured out her soul to the Lord. She told him not to take her for a wicked woman—she had been praying out of her great anguish and grief.

 Eli told her to go in peace and prayed the Lord would grant her what she had asked of Him. Hannah went home with her husband to worship and the Lord remembered her. In time, she became pregnant with a son and she named him Samuel, which means "heard by God."

Hannah kept her promise, and after the boy was weaned, she took him to the priest to serve and honor the Lord with his whole life. Hannah prayed for him, entrusted him to the priest, and returned home. God was gracious to Hannah. After she kept her promise, she and her husband went from a barren womb to three more sons and two daughters, while Samuel continued to grow up in the presence of the Lord as he served Eli the priest.

Eli had his own sons who served as priests, but they were wicked and abused their responsibilities, offending God and the people. A man of God came to Eli and told him God had given him a message about his sons. Because of their disobedience, they would be judged.

And then one night, God began to speak directly to this little boy who had been placed in Eli's care.

> ## 1 Samuel 1:19b-20
>
> [19] . . . and the Lord remembered her. [20] So in the course of time Hannah became pregnant and gave birth to a son. She named him Samuel, saying, "Because I asked the Lord for him."

1 SAMUEL 3:1-21 (NIV)

[1] The boy Samuel ministered before the Lord under Eli. In those days the word of the Lord was rare; there were not many visions.

[2] One night Eli, whose eyes were becoming so weak that he could barely see, was lying down in his usual place. [3] The lamp of God had not yet gone out, and Samuel was lying down in the house of the Lord, where the ark of God was. [4] Then the Lord called Samuel.

Samuel answered, "Here I am." [5] And he ran to Eli and said, "Here I am; you called me."

But Eli said, "I did not call; go back and lie down." So he went and lay down.

[6] Again the Lord called, "Samuel!" And Samuel got up and went to Eli and said, "Here I am; you called me."

"My son," Eli said, "I did not call; go back and lie down."

[7] Now Samuel did not yet know the Lord: The word of the Lord had not yet been revealed to him.

[8] A third time the Lord called, "Samuel!" And Samuel got up and went to Eli and said, "Here I am; you called me."

Then Eli realized that the Lord was calling the boy. [9] So Eli told Samuel, "Go and lie down, and if he calls you, say, 'Speak, Lord, for your servant is listening.'" So Samuel went and lay down in his place.

[10] The Lord came and stood there, calling as at the other times, "Samuel! Samuel!"

Then Samuel said, "Speak, for your servant is listening."

Samuel! Samuel!

1 SAMUEL 3:1-21 (NIV) CONTD.

[11] And the Lord said to Samuel: "See, I am about to do something in Israel that will make the ears of everyone who hears about it tingle. [12] At that time I will carry out against Eli everything I spoke against his family—from beginning to end. [13] For I told him that I would judge his family forever because of the sin he knew about; his sons blasphemed God, and he failed to restrain them. [14] Therefore I swore to the house of Eli, 'The guilt of Eli's house will never be atoned for by sacrifice or offering.'"

[15] Samuel lay down until morning and then opened the doors of the house of the Lord. He was afraid to tell Eli the vision, [16] but Eli called him and said, "Samuel, my son."

Samuel answered, "Here I am."

[17] "What was it he said to you?" Eli asked. "Do not hide it from me. May God deal with you, be it ever so severely, if you hide from me anything he told you." [18] So Samuel told him everything, hiding nothing from him. Then Eli said, "He is the Lord; let him do what is good in his eyes."

[19] The Lord was with Samuel as he grew up, and he let none of Samuel's words fall to the ground. [20] And all Israel from Dan to Beersheba recognized that Samuel was attested as a prophet of the Lord. [21] The Lord continued to appear at Shiloh, and there he revealed himself to Samuel through his word.

He is the Lord...

WHAT DOES THIS MEAN FOR US?

Samuel's story shows us the relational nature of hearing God. Samuel was aware and listening. When his name was called, he got up and answered. And when God spoke to Samuel, even though it was difficult, he obeyed.

 This is a great reminder for all of us. We have learned God is a communicator, He has given us the privilege of hearing His voice, and so as His people, His sheep, we should be ready to listen. And when we hear Him, we demonstrate our love for Him through our obedience.

It's not only when we read the Bible, pray, or attend a worship service with our family—God can, and will, speak to us while we're at work, while we're driving in the car, while we're doing dishes, when we lay down at night, or when we're out on a walk.

John 14:21

"Whoever has my commands and keeps them is the one who loves me. The one who loves me will be loved by my Father, and I too will love them and show myself to them."

He doesn't speak more to people who know more spiritual information. He speaks to people ready to listen. We can all grow in this area.

Truth is less propositional, less about information, and much more about a relationship with a person.

This is why we should approach God's Word with a simple prayer like: Lord, I want to know You. I'm ready to listen. Please speak to me through Your Word so I can know and love You more.

It's a prayer He will always answer.

In Jesus, we get the best of both worlds. We get the power of an intimate, personal relationship with God like Samuel had. But we also get something he never had. Something Samuel would have loved. We get the complete Word of God available to us at any moment.

 Every word in Scripture is intentional, meaningful, and chosen by the inspiration of the Holy Spirit. There is great value in memorizing and knowing the Word. But reading the Bible is less about acquiring spiritual information and more about spending time with Jesus (the Living Word) who renews our minds and transforms our hearts.

> ### 2 Timothy 3:16-17
>
> [16] All Scripture is God-breathed and is useful for teaching, rebuking, correcting and training in righteousness, [17] so that the servant may be thoroughly equipped for every good work.

WHAT DO I DO WITH THIS?

Developing a relationship with someone requires consistent correspondence. While it may not be like the excitement of spontaneity, it produces a genuine connection.

This requires a measure of commitment and discipline.
- Do you have a regular time and place to hear from God?
- If He was looking for you, would He know where to find you?
- When was the last time you asked to meet with Him?

We're all busy with overscheduled lives and this sounds like one more thing we don't have time for. But we all make time for the things that matter the most.

It doesn't have to be a full hour of power … but that's a great goal to shoot for. The most important thing is to get started with a regular time and place.

Five minutes every day is a great place to start. You're going to do *something* with those five minutes. What could be more valuable than hearing from God?

TO HELP YOU GET TRACTION:

1 Set a reminder/alarm for a specific time.

2 Choose a specific place where you can sit undistracted and put all of your attention and focus on God.

3 Start with the simple prayer mentioned on page 37.

4 If you've never read the Bible, start by reading through the Gospel of John. Once you've finished John, read the other Gospels (Matthew, Mark, and Luke) **or** read one chapter of Proverbs and one Psalm each day.

5 Finish with a simple prayer thanking God for His Word and for speaking to you.

6 As five minutes becomes routine, see if you can make it ten, then fifteen, etc.

GOD SPEAKS THROUGH HIS WORD, SO WE REGULARLY READ THE BIBLE.

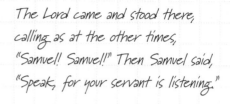

The Lord came and stood there,
calling as at the other times,
"Samuel! Samuel!" Then Samuel said,
"Speak, for your servant is listening."

1 Samuel 3:10

1 SAMUEL 3:10 (NIV)

The Lord came and
stood there, calling as
at the other times,
"Samuel! Samuel!"

Then Samuel said,
*"Speak, for your servant
is listening."*

MEMORY VERSE

DISCUSSION QUESTIONS

1. Have you ever felt God speak to you before? What was that like?

2. Read 1 Samuel 3:8-10. Why do you think God repeatedly calls out to Samuel?

3. Samuel's response in verse 10 is so simple. What does his response teach us about hearing from God?

4. How can we position ourselves to hear God's voice more?

5. One of the ways we hear from God is by reading the Bible. Why are commitment and discipline necessary to read God's Word?

6. The purpose of reading the Bible is relational, not informational. How does this affect the way you read your Bible?

7. Do you have a regular time and place to hear from God? Explain.

8. What are the benefits of having a set time and place to hear from God?

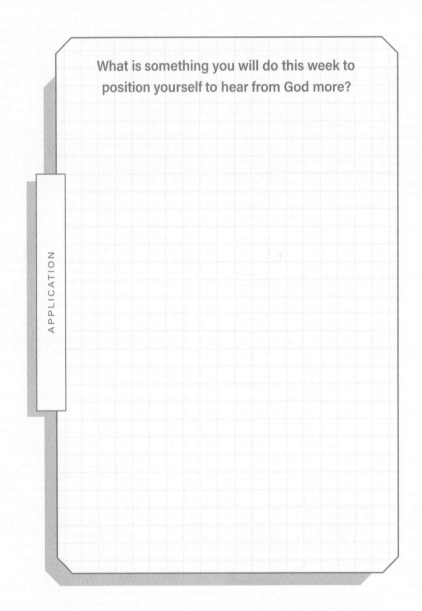

What is something you will do this week to position yourself to hear from God more?

APPLICATION

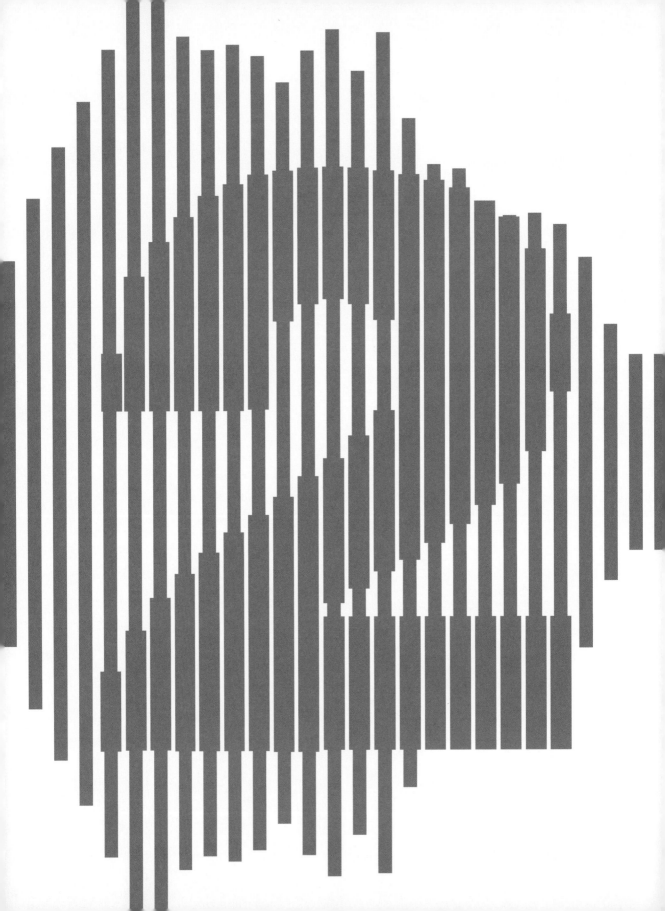

GOD SPEAKS THROUGH PATTERNS & PRINCIPLES IN HIS WORD

CONCEPT

Let's be honest. Here's the stuff we really want the Bible to tell us:

- Am I supposed to take this job?
- Should I marry this person?
- Who am I supposed to vote for?
- How do I get my spouse to respect me?
- Do I eat gluten? Dairy? Meat?
- Why won't my teenager listen to me?

We want the Bible to be like the back of our high school math textbook. What's the answer to #4?

While God's Word is filled with wisdom that applies to every area of our lives, it's not designed like a rule book to neatly and efficiently address all of life's decisions.

The purpose of God's Word is to show us who God is, to reveal His character and nature, to invite us into a relationship with Him, and then to show us how to live.

The order is important.

The purpose of God's Word is.....

There is no doubt this approach takes longer, but it is more holistic and relational. In the long run, it is much more valuable.

God does not just give us answers to life's questions—He gives us Himself. This is so much better.

More than a judge rendering verdicts and decisions, God is a loving Father who works patiently with us as we move through life. He does not give up on us when we choose not to listen to His voice, make the wrong choice, or give in to temptation.

 He doesn't expect us to be perfect, but He wants us to make progress. Philippians 1:6 says the same God who began a good work in us will be faithful to complete it until the day of Christ Jesus. In other words, as long as we're alive, God will keep working in us. We never arrive and we never outgrow the need to listen to His voice and apply His Word to our lives.

He is more concerned with who we are becoming than what we are doing.

And we grow in our understanding of who God is, who we are, and who we are becoming by regularly reading and applying His Word.

> **Philippians 1:6**
>
> . . . being confident of this, that he who began a good work in you will carry it on to completion until the day of Christ Jesus.

God never contradicts Himself or violates His Word. What He says, He means. What He means, He does.

IF WE THINK WE HEAR SOMETHING FROM GOD THAT VIOLATES THE CONSISTENT MESSAGE OF HIS WORD, WE CAN BE CERTAIN IT'S NOT GOD.

If you hear a voice in your head saying, *It's just business. It's okay for you to break the law to close this deal because it's so lucrative,* it's not God. You don't have to pray about it.

If you hear a voice in your head saying, *Your spouse isn't making you happy. You fell out of love. It happens. This other person understands you and you have real chemistry. You both married the wrong person but if you come together, you'll finally be happy!* This isn't God either.

Don't look for someone who will agree with those feelings. Don't follow your heart. Don't live your truth. None of these feelings line up with God's Word, so you know they're not from Him.

These thoughts are simple to dismiss because they're both so clearly defined in the Word. It gets more difficult when the lines aren't so clear.

But as we grow in our understanding of the Word, we'll be able to apply His principles to any situation we find ourselves in. And the best way to grow in our understanding is to learn how to read, interpret, and apply the Bible in a healthy way.

Remember, the purpose of the Bible is to show us who God is. More than a series of disconnected stories and types of ancient literature, the Bible is one story that always points us to the person of Jesus.

For example, the Bible is divided into the Old Testament (or old covenant) and the New Testament (or new covenant).

The Old Testament explains how God created human beings in order to be with them, how humans disobeyed and broke the relationship, and how God worked through imperfect people toward His plan to redeem and restore all of mankind. Everything in the Old Testament shows mankind's brokenness and need for a Savior in order to be restored to God. It all points to Jesus.

The New Testament tells the story of how Jesus, the Son of God, the Living Word, came into our world to show us what God is like. He announced the long-awaited arrival of God's Kingdom, served, preached, performed miracles, and came to seek and save the lost. He lived a perfect life in our place and died a criminal's death to satisfy a payment we owed but could never pay. Through His death and resurrection, He restored peace between God and humans, entrusted His mission to His disciples, and established the Church as His covenant people in the earth.

When we understand this big-picture arc of the Bible, we can properly understand all of the smaller stories, moments, and characters in the Bible through that lens.

One of the most common mistakes people make in misunderstanding Scripture is reading it out of context. They pull words, phrases, verses, stories, chapters, or even books of the Bible out of context to make them mean something other than what the Bible actually says.

We always read the Bible in context. There are several different types of context:

- **Historical Context** — What was happening in the world when this passage was written?
- **Cultural Context** — How did their language, customs, and traditions shape the way they understood what was happening?

- **Literary Context** — What kind of literature is this book in the Bible (narrative, poetry, wisdom, etc.), and how does one part fit within the greater message of the Bible?

This can be intimidating. It could make you feel like you have to be a Bible scholar to read or understand God's Word.

That's not the case. When you read the Bible, one of the first and most surprising things you'll realize is how much we have in common with these people who lived thousands of years ago.

They often feel what we feel. They think the way we think.

Remember, we're learning about hearing God. This is more about our relationship with God than how much spiritual information we know.

But it will help us to remember these words in the Bible were written to real people, in a real place, through the inspiration of a real God.

When we have the attitude of a learner, when we come trusting God to help us understand, we position ourselves to hear Him more clearly.

If we're willing to ask context questions like, *What did it mean to them?*, *How did they think about their world?*, and *What kind of writing is this?* before we jump to *What does this mean to me?*, we will hear God much more clearly.

In the same way, when we learn a new skill in any area of our lives, with consistent application, we'll grow more proficient over time.

CONTEXT

Timothy was a significant leader in the early church. Both his mother and grandmother were people of faith who taught him to love God from an early age, and then the apostle Paul became a spiritual father to him.

He led the Church in Ephesus, one of the more significant churches in the ancient world. The church faced many challenges and controversies. Ephesus was home to one of the seven wonders of the ancient world, the Temple of Artemis.

It was a wealthy city and the temple generated a lot of worship and wealth for the people. When people gave their lives to Christ and stopped worshiping false gods, a riot broke out.

Toward the end of Paul's life, he was in prison in Rome awaiting trial and his eventual execution. He sent a letter to Timothy which was his final instruction and encouragement for his spiritual son to stay faithful to the call of God on his life and to stand up to people who misrepresented God and His Word.

2 Timothy 1:5

I am reminded of your sincere faith, which first lived in your grandmother Lois and in your mother Eunice and, I am persuaded, now lives in you also.

2 TIMOTHY 3:14-17 (NIV)

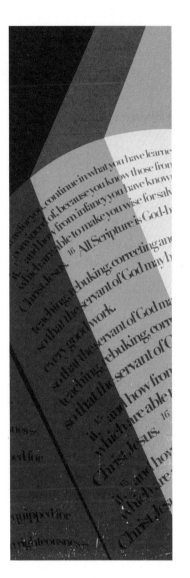

[14] But as for you, continue in what you have learned and have become convinced of, because you know those from whom you learned it, [15] and how from infancy you have known the Holy Scriptures, which are able to make you wise for salvation through faith in Christ Jesus.

[16] All Scripture is God-breathed and is useful for teaching, rebuking, correcting and training in righteousness, [17] so that the servant of God may be thoroughly equipped for every good work.

. . . equipped for every good work.

WHAT DOES THIS MEAN FOR US?

Remember the nature of Paul's relationship with Timothy. He was a spiritual father to him, which means he was deeply and personally invested in Timothy's success.

Timothy was leading the church in Ephesus, one of the larger and more influential churches in the ancient world, and the city was filled with tension and adversity. Paul believed in Timothy and gave him every bit of Spirit-led wisdom he could, but he also knew he couldn't solve Timothy's problems for him. Some of Timothy's growth and progress would come through making the best decision he could based on God's Word and dealing with the consequences.

Paul points Timothy back to the confidence he had in God, in what he believed with conviction, and the power of the Holy Scriptures, the Word of God. He reminds his son in the Lord that the entire Bible (all Scripture) has been breathed on and inspired by God and therefore is useful for teaching, challenging mindsets, developing character, and growing in spiritual and emotional maturity.

Because of this, there is no area of our lives where this growth process leaves us unprepared.

The Bible does not give us every answer to every personal and difficult question we face in life. But a consistent and dynamic relationship with the Word of God will make us thoroughly equipped for every good work.

In other words, God has given us everything we need to hear His voice, obey, and live the life we've been created to live.

Peter said it this way in 2 Peter 1:3: "His divine power has given us everything we need for a godly life through our knowledge of him who called us by his own glory and goodness."

WHAT DO I DO WITH THIS?

The Bible is a library of 66 books written over a span of approximately 1,500 years by more than 40 authors under the supervision and inspiration of the Holy Spirit.

This can be challenging for us, but it is the key to learning how to hear the voice of God.

Reading, studying, and understanding God's Word is not something we solve in a guide like this. It's a lifelong journey for every follower of Christ. All of us can grow in our understanding of God and His Word.

We designed this guide to help each of us take our next step. Don't get discouraged with what you don't know—be inspired to keep growing.

The Bible is a library of

66 books

written over a span of approximately 1,500 years

by more than 40 authors

under the supervision
and inspiration of the Holy Spirit.

Here are few things that can help:

The "**SOAP**" method is a helpful tool for learning to study the Bible. It stands for **S**cripture, **O**bservation, **A**pplication, and **P**rayer.

Scripture – Start with reading a small portion of Scripture (a chapter per day is a great way to start). If you've never read the Bible, start in the Gospel of John in the New Testament. Remember, we don't read the Bible as disconnected chunks, but as one big story that always points us to Jesus.

Observation – Ask simple questions of the passage: Who are the characters? What are the challenges they're facing? What do they do? What does Jesus say to them?

Application – What does this mean to you? How does what Jesus say to them fit with the big story of Scripture? What would it look like for you to live this way?

Prayer – In your own words, ask God to help you live this out and hear Him more clearly.

If you want to get better at reading the Bible as one big story, *The Jesus Storybook Bible* is really helpful, even if you don't have kids. You could also try *The Story*, which is an abridged version of the Bible put into chronological order. Perhaps the most well-known Bible paraphrase is *The Message*, which takes the entire Bible and puts it into contemporary language.

These resources are called "paraphrases," because the writers summarize and simplify the message of the Bible to help us understand them better. A translation is when a group of scholars carefully go back to the original language and select the best words to give us the closest interpretation of the Bible.

Paraphrases increase our understanding, but our regular Bible reading should be with a sound translation of Scripture.

If you want to learn more about the cultural and historical context of the Bible or more significant details, both the *NIV Study Bible* and the *ESV Study Bible* (both edited by D.A. Carson) are very helpful.

Remember, whether we're new to the Bible or we've been faithfully reading for decades, we read to know and hear God's voice. When we ask Him, we can have confidence He'll speak to us through His Word.

GOD SPEAKS THROUGH PATTERNS AND PRINCIPLES IN HIS WORD, SO WE TAKE STEPS TO KEEP GROWING IN OUR UNDERSTANDING OF SCRIPTURE.

Use this space to write down the memory verse. If you do this multiple times each week, it will help you memorize it.

2 TIMOTHY 3:16 (NIV)

All Scripture is God-breathed and is useful for teaching, rebuking, correcting and training in righteousness.

MEMORY VERSE

1. Read 2 Timothy 3:16. According to this verse, what is the Bible useful for? Write down all four concepts Paul mentions. Then discuss how the Bible accomplishes each of these concepts.

2. Read 2 Timothy 3:17. According to this verse, what is the outcome of studying God's Word?

3. How does the Bible equip us for "every good work"? What does that mean?

4. Why is knowing the big story of the Bible important? How well do you know that story?

5. The purpose of God's Word is to reveal God's character and nature to us and to invite us into a relationship with Him. How does knowing this affect how you read the Bible?

6. Last week, we talked about having a set time and place to read God's Word. What should that time look like? What does it look like for you when you study the Bible?

7. Use the S.O.A.P. method to study a passage of Scripture. If you need more space, you can use page 67.
S - Scripture - Read James 1:22-25.
O - Observation - What observations can you make from the text?
A - Application - How can you apply these verses to your life?
P - Prayer - In your own words, write out a simple prayer to God based on what you learned from this text.

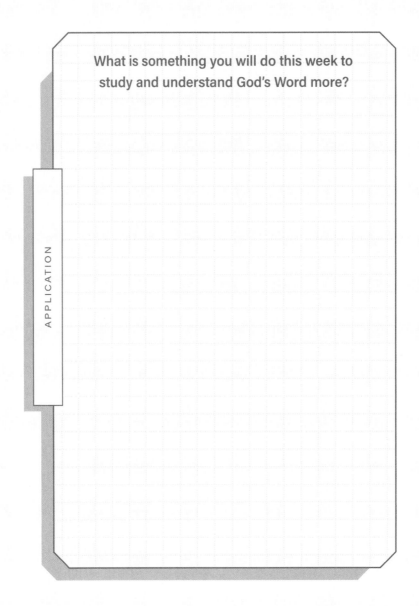

What is something you will do this week to study and understand God's Word more?

APPLICATION

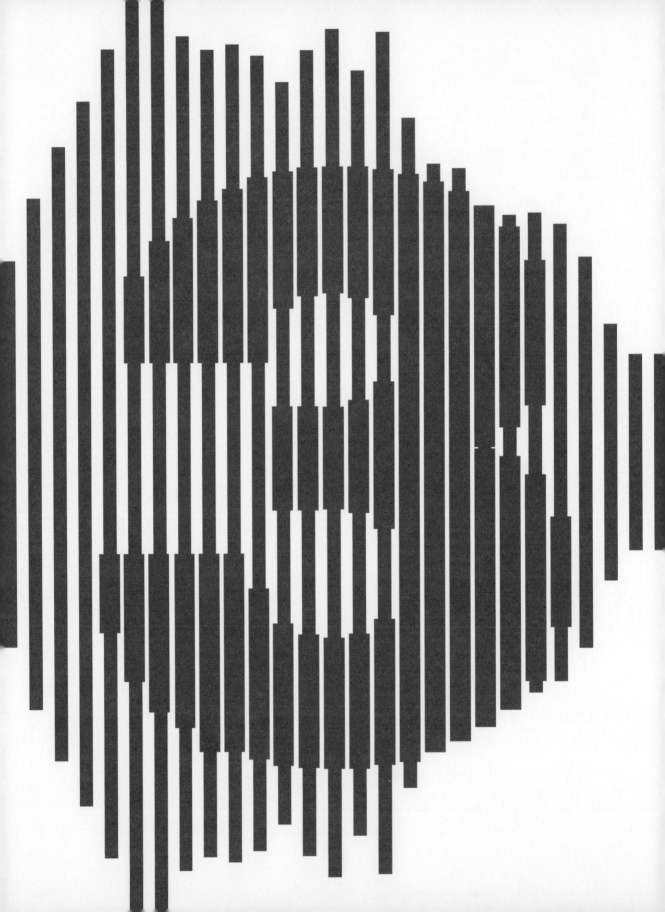

WEEK THREE

GOD SPEAKS THROUGH THE HOLY SPIRIT

CONCEPT

Jesus shows us what God is like.

The Word helps us learn to hear God.

And the principles of the Word give us the wisdom we need to make good decisions in every area of our lives.

So far, so good.

Hearing God is not easy, and we feel pressure because we know it's important, but at least each of these makes sense. We can look at the words, think about their meaning, and find clarity.

But if we're honest . . . most of us aren't sure what to make of the Holy Spirit.

How do you learn to relate to a "Spirit"? This doesn't come naturally to us. We're not even sure how to talk about it. It's uncomfortable.

The good news is that Jesus anticipated our struggle and gave us everything we need to have a meaningful and genuine relationship with the Holy Spirit.

He actually told the disciples it was for their good (and ours) that He was going back to the Father. He said it would be to their advantage (and ours) if He left. Why?

JESUS SENDS US THE HOLY SPIRIT, THE ADVOCATE, THE HELPER, TO BE WITH US.

Notice in John 16:7, when Jesus refers to the Holy Spirit, He says "Him" not "it." This is an important detail. The Holy Spirit is a person. He is fully God. He is more than a feeling, an expressive type of worship service, or an excuse to act crazy in church.

Some people feel cautious about Him because they've seen things they didn't understand. Other people are reluctant to find out more because they come from a tradition or background where people were concerned about this conversation.

John 16:7

"But very truly I tell you, it is for your good that I am going away. Unless I go away, the Advocate will not come to you; but if I go, I will send him to you."

The majority of people are unaware, meaning they simply haven't thought much about it or looked into it for themselves.

While it may take a little getting used to and require you to reconsider what someone else may have told you, if you can relate to Jesus through God's Word, you can learn to relate to the Holy Spirit.

Jesus is excited for you to receive this advantage—to experience the benefits of the promise of the supernatural help that comes from a relationship with the Holy Spirit.

When Jesus first told His disciples about the Holy Spirit in John 14, He called Him the Spirit of truth and He told them He would help them and be with them forever. A few moments later, He explained the Spirit of truth would teach them all things and remind them of everything Jesus had said to them.

The Holy Spirit did it for them and He'll do it for us too.

Have you ever been in a situation where you thought, *I know I've read something in the Bible that speaks to this issue, but I can't remember where.* We've all been there. And in those moments, it's the Holy Spirit who reminds us through a voice, a thought, or the help of a friend.

Sounds pretty good, doesn't it? He's way better than Google or Alexa.

John 14:16-17a

16 "And I will ask the Father, and he will give you another advocate to help you and be with you forever— 17a the Spirit of truth."

John 14:26

"But the Advocate, the Holy Spirit, whom the Father will send in my name, will teach you all things and will remind you of everything I have said to you."

CONTEXT

It's one of the most important and emotionally charged moments in the entire Bible. Jesus is sharing the last supper He would have with His disciples before He would be betrayed, arrested, beaten, and crucified. He is preparing them for the stark reality they are about to face in a matter of hours.

They are about to lose everything they have spent the last few years building. They will watch helplessly as their closest Friend, their Lord, the One they have given up everything to follow, is savagely and publicly tortured.

They too will be mocked and humiliated, they will watch Him die, and then because they don't know what else to do, they'll try to return to their old lives.

Jesus knows His friends are about to go through something incredibly difficult and traumatic. He knows how much fear, anxiety, guilt, and shame they are about to endure.

In the garden, He would pray for them and ask the Father to strengthen them, but with His words, He inspires them with the confidence and hope they would receive through the power of the Spirit.

Even though He knew the incredible challenges and adversity they were about to face, He still believed they could take up His mission, advance His Kingdom, build His Church, and change the world.

He believed this because He knew the Holy Spirit would be with them to help them.

. . . he will make known to you.

JOHN 16:12-15 (NIV)

[12] "I have much more to say to you, more than you can now bear. [13] But when he, the Spirit of truth, comes, he will guide you into all the truth. He will not speak on his own; he will speak only what he hears, and he will tell you what is yet to come. [14] He will glorify me because it is from me that he will receive what he will make known to you. [15] All that belongs to the Father is mine. That is why I said the Spirit will receive from me what he will make known to you."

. . . he will guide you into all truth.

WHAT DOES THIS MEAN FOR US?

What an interesting detail John gives us in verse 12 that we could easily pass right over. He has more to say to us than we can handle.

It's a common theme He continually repeats. Jesus' primary goal is not to give us all the spiritual information possible. He gives us what we can effectively process and obey.

Learning to hear from God always comes back to, "Did you do what He already told you?" We want to hear something new. Jesus always comes back to, "If you love Me, obey what I told you."

Next, we see that the Spirit will guide us into all truth. Not some things. Not only spiritual things. All the things. Whatever we're willing to ask. Whatever we have ears to hear.

And then finally, Jesus gives us such a clear picture of what the Spirit

> **John 16:12**
>
> "I have much more to say to you, more than you can now bear."

does. He constantly reinforces the relationship between the Father and the Son, glorifying them through reminding and revealing their hearts for us.

Remember, the goal of hearing from God is less about getting the information we're looking for and much more about understanding who God is, how He loves us, and how His goodness and love change every relationship we have.

The question is not whether the Holy Spirit speaks to us on a daily basis. Jesus told us He'd always be with us, He'd never leave us, and He would guide us into all truth.

But typically, He doesn't tell us the next thing until we listen to the last thing He said. He's looking for our cooperation, our openness, and our gratitude for His voice expressed not through our perfection but our willingness to listen.

 There is a pattern in the New Testament where the authors would follow Jesus' example and quote Scripture from the Old Testament. For example, Hebrews 3:7-8 quotes Psalm 95:8: "Today, if you hear his voice, do not harden your hearts ..."

The author quotes this passage because there's also a pattern when God speaks, instead of listening and obeying, the people harden their hearts and turn from Him.

Hebrews 3:7-8

[7] So, as the Holy Spirit says: "Today, if you hear his voice, [8] do not harden your hearts as you did in the rebellion, during the time of testing in the wilderness."

Will you trust Him by listening with a tender and open heart? Will you receive what He says to you with gratitude or will you counter with your own offer in an attempt to get your way?

Hearing God is less about questions and answers and more about being invited into an eternal, loving conversation between the Father, the Son, and the Spirit. Each member of the Trinity is others-focused with self-giving love out of their reverence and honor for one another.

And through the Spirit of God, we're invited into this self-giving, others-focused way of life, which should impact how we relate to everyone else in our lives.

None of us adjust to this right away. It's a process that takes time. But as you follow the disciples through the book of Acts and later into their letters, you see them soften and grow in the way they love and serve others because of the power of the Holy Spirit working in their lives.

The same process should take place in our lives too as we grow in our relationship with the same Holy Spirit.

WHAT DO I DO WITH THIS?

How do you learn to hear from the Holy Spirit? You ask.

Jesus told us how it works in Luke 11:13: "If you then, though you are evil, know how to give good gifts to your children, how much more will your Father in heaven give the Holy Spirit to those who ask him!"

When was the last time you asked the Holy Spirit to speak to you?

You may not have even realized this was something you could do. Jesus makes it so simple.

When we ask, when we listen, and when we acknowledge His constant presence in our lives, He leads us into all truth and reminds us of everything Jesus said.

You might be wondering, *How will I know it's Him?*

Remember, He doesn't speak on His own out of nowhere. He passes on what the Father and the Son have said.

When you have a challenge with your spouse, one of your children, a friend, or a co-worker, your thoughts and attitude will remind you of all the ways they've mistreated you.

The Holy Spirit won't start with them. He will lovingly start with you.
- How could you be more loving?
- How could you offer grace and kindness?
- Instead of being right or making your point, what does Jesus want you to say?

When you take this posture, it may not be immediate, it probably won't happen the way you expect, but you will see the Holy Spirit intervene and bring His healing power into these situations.

GOD SPEAKS THROUGH THE HOLY SPIRIT, SO WE CAN REMEMBER WHAT JESUS SAID AND BE GUIDED INTO ALL TRUTH.

JOHN 14:26 (NIV)

"But the Advocate,
the Holy Spirit,
whom the Father
will send in my name,
will teach you
all things and will
remind you of
everything I have
said to you."

DISCUSSION QUESTIONS

1. Read John 14:16-17a. How does Jesus describe the Holy Spirit in these verses? What do you think these terms mean?

2. According to these verses, why did Jesus say He would send the Holy Spirit? Why is this important?

3. How often do you ask the Holy Spirit to help you or be with you? Explain.

4. Read John 14:26. What does Jesus say the Holy Spirit will do for us? Why is this important when hearing from God?

5. How does the Holy Spirit illuminate God's Word to us today?

6. The Holy Spirit wants to speak, but we have to be willing to listen and obey what He says. Why is obedience tied to hearing from God?

7. Is there something God has told you to do recently? If so, what is it, and are you obeying what He said?

8. Read Luke 11:13. Are you in the habit of asking the Holy Spirit to speak to you? Explain.

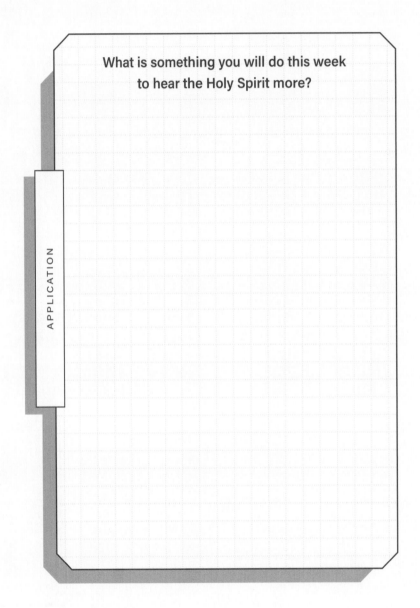

**What is something you will do this week
to hear the Holy Spirit more?**

APPLICATION

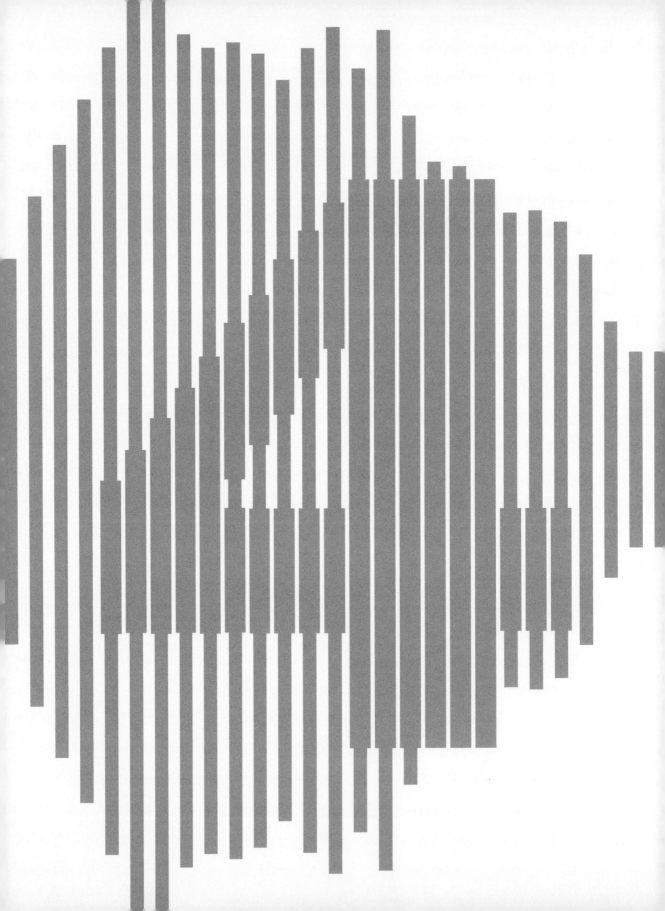

GOD SPEAKS THROUGH TRUSTED VOICES

CONCEPT

We've never had more voices speaking to us at the same time.

*THE COMPETITION FOR OUR ATTENTION HAS NEVER BEEN SO INTENSE.

The stakes are high. The brightest minds are constantly thinking of ways to hook us because they know our attention is valuable and they can monetize anything we watch, skim, search, read, or listen to.

We used to read books or magazines—now we "scroll" on our phones … and it's a scroll that never ends. More content is uploaded every day than we'll ever be able to see.

We used to watch television—now we "binge" streaming services, but there are so many to choose from, it feels like we'll never catch up to what everyone else is talking about.

Our cares and concerns used to be largely limited to what was happening in our community—now we get real-time updates from all over the world.

There are so many voices all clamoring for our attention. Most of the things vying for our notice present themselves as life-and-death issues genuinely worthy of our deepest worries.

In reality, the majority are so inconsequential that we won't remember them in a week. Unsolicited junk mail used to be confined to the mailbox, but now it feels like it has followed us into every area of our lives.

Once we reduce these voices down to the ones that actually matter, we're still not done. At this point, we're left to discern which voices are wise and life-giving and which voices are deceitful and dangerous.

How can we tell the difference? How do we sift through the noise to find the things that are genuinely meaningful?

There's a simple and effective three-word phrase that can help us in these moments: **Consider the source.**

As we discovered in the introduction, the first humans walked and talked with God on a daily basis.[1] It was part of their routine. Their relationship was perfect until an outside adversary poisoned their trust by questioning both God's words and His motives.

When this happened, for the first time in history, humans hid from God because they were naked and afraid. This is silly because you can't hide from God; He sees and knows everything.[2]

But because God loved them, He didn't let them stay "hidden." He wanted them to realize and own what they had done. So when Adam explained what happened, God simply asked, "Who told you . . . ?"

In other words, the voices we listen to determine what we hear. And who we listen to changes how we hear.

What and *how* depend on *who*.

Proverbs 12:15 says, "The way of fools seems right to them, but the wise listen to advice."

We often give ourselves too much credit. We think of ourselves as rational, thoughtful beings. The truth is, most of us decide what we want, and then we try to rationalize a reason why it's the right choice.

Our minds attempt to justify what our hearts desire. We would rather find someone to agree with us than challenge our thought process.

> **Genesis 3:8-11**
>
> [8] Then the man and his wife heard the sound of the Lord God as he was walking in the garden in the cool of the day, and they hid from the Lord God among the trees of the garden. [9] But the Lord God called to the man, "Where are you?" [10] He answered, "I heard you in the garden, and I was afraid because I was naked; so I hid." [11] And he said, "Who told you that you were naked? Have you eaten from the tree that I commanded you not to eat from?"

---

1 Remember, this story comes from all the way back in Genesis 3.

2 See Psalm 139:1-12 and 1 Corinthians 4:5 to start. There are many more examples.

Science calls this approach *confirmation bias.*

Unfortunately, this is a theme all throughout Scripture. God speaks to His people but they don't listen. When God speaks to His people through Jeremiah in chapter 6 verse 10, He says, "To whom can I speak and give warning? Who will listen to me? Their ears are closed so they cannot hear. The word of the Lord is offensive to them; they find no pleasure in it."

This is a fairly accurate summary of the Old Testament.

God has a better way for us.

He brings people into our lives who know and trust His voice. When they speak, we need to listen. They don't just tell us what to do. They show us how to recognize and respond to God. Wise and trusted voices give us more than rules and platitudes—they help us learn to hear God ourselves.

Proverbs 13:20 tells us, "Walk with the wise and become wise, for a companion of fools suffers harm."

God has a better way for us.

CONTEXT

Matthew 5-7 is one of the most unique passages in the entire Bible. You may have heard it called "The Sermon on the Mount."

It's given this name because large crowds of people came from all over the region to hear Jesus, so He went up on a small mountain to use the natural amplification to help all the people hear His words.

The latter portion of Chapter 7 is the end of the longest single message in the Bible. It's also the most famous message ever preached.

How does Jesus end His message? He's given all this teaching, but He turns their attention to focusing on themselves and their own spiritual growth.

- Don't worry about everyone else. Are you growing closer to God and obeying Him?
- If you ask, seek, and knock, God will open the door and answer you. He's not hiding from you. He wants to speak to you.
- There are two options—a wide path to destruction, and

a narrow path that leads to life. Don't go wide; stay narrow.

· There are true and false teachers, sheep and wolves, good trees and bad trees, and true and false disciples.

· Don't blame someone else for the choices you make. You have been given everything you need to make the right choice and to follow Jesus.

This is how He sets up His close. But how does He bring it home? What's the last thing Jesus says?

...puts them into practice

MATTHEW 7:24-27 (NIV)

24 "Therefore everyone who hears these words of mine and puts them into practice is like a wise man who built his house on the rock. 25 The rain came down, the streams rose, and the winds blew and beat against that house; yet it did not fall, because it had its foundation on the rock. 26 But everyone who hears these words of mine and does not put them into practice is like a foolish man who built his house on sand. 27 The rain came down, the streams rose, and the winds blew and beat against that house, and it fell with a great crash."

...yet it did not fall.

CAUTION

By this point, we've established we learn to hear and trust God's voice through His Word. **Get ready—this is an area where this WILL be tested!**

Because most human beings are more led by their feelings than their convictions, well-meaning people will often say things like, "I feel like God wants you to be happy!"

It may sound loving and compassionate, but it's dangerous. It's a trap.

This sentiment can be used to excuse everything from choosing not to forgive someone who hurt you, compromising your integrity at work, being unfaithful with your spouse, neglecting to discipline your children, or failing to honor God with your resources.

No matter what anyone else says, these feelings do not line up with God's Word, so we can be certain this is NOT what He is saying.

Once we've decided what we want, our human nature convinces us to search for voices who will affirm our choices instead of leaning into the trusted voices who love us enough to tell us the truth according to God's Word.

Wise people who hear God don't start with, "Agree with me." They always start with, "Remind me of God's Word."

WHAT DOES THIS MEAN FOR US?

You don't get a spiritual trophy for showing up. You don't get an attendance award just for listening to the words of Jesus. That's not the goal. It's bigger than spiritual content.

Jesus said not to just hear His words … but to put them into practice. Practice doesn't mean perfect. He doesn't expect you to be perfect every time, but He does expect you to make progress.

We think the problem is not having enough information. We tell ourselves that if we keep looking, we can learn everything we need. That's not what Jesus says.

The foolish builder's issue was not a lack of information. He heard the same words as his wise counterpart. The real problem is obedience. He knew what to do but he chose not to do it.

If we're honest, we struggle with this too. The typical follower of Christ is educated beyond their level of obedience.

Notice also, we don't get a great indicator of what we've built on when the sun is shining and everything in our lives is great. **We discover what we built on when the storms of life come.**

The rain starts pounding against our foundation, the water starts to rise, and we get afraid and upset. And whatever is in our hearts starts to come out of our mouths.

What separates the wise person from the fool? Is it a lack of rain? Is it fewer storms? Nope. It all comes down to how we respond to the storms.

When everything in life starts to fall apart—you have a health scare, you go through major career challenges, you feel taken advantage of at work and underappreciated in your home—now you're going to see what you built on.

The wise person builds on the rock of the revelation of Jesus. Which voices do we trust? Which voices do we prioritize? The voices who point us to Jesus.

He's not reactionary, motivated by fear, or operating with a scarcity mindset.

Jesus is not in a hurry. He leads us; He doesn't drive us. We listen for His voice and trust Him.

Humans are relational beings. Without even trying, we take on the qualities and the attitudes of the people we're surrounded by.

IT'S IMPORTANT TO LEAN INTO THE TRUSTED VOICES IN OUR LIVES WHO REMIND US OF WHAT JESUS HAS SAID.

We become like the people we listen to. We value what they value. We move in the same direction they're moving because we share common goals and values.

This is where the old saying comes from: **Show me your friends, and I'll show you your future.**

This is why it's important for us to love everyone while also carefully considering the voices we give influence to. We have to be intentional to tune out foolishness and amplify wisdom in our lives.

WHAT DO I DO WITH THIS?

This same principle applies to learning skills and developing abilities in other areas of our lives.

If you want to start a business, if you want to learn a language, if you want to become a better spouse or parent, if you want to fix things around the house, find someone who knows how to do it and listen to them.

You're not looking for someone who's perfect—those are impossible to find. But you also don't treat everyone's opinion equally.

- Do they know God's Word?
- Do they put it into practice?
- Can you see their progress and growth?
- Do they encourage you to align your decisions with the authority of God's Word?
- Do they inspire you to grow in your faith and keep taking steps in your understanding?

Being a part of a church is more than attending services. This is why we emphasize getting connected, taking steps, serving, and regularly being part of a Small Group.

This is what the Church does—we grow together as a spiritual family, asking God to speak to us, and obeying Him when He does.

If we want our kids to live this way, one of the best ways for them to learn is to watch us as parents model it in front of them. The best pastors, mentors, and Small Group leaders don't make our choices for us. They teach us how to hear from God, encourage us to process what we're hearing, and then obey the best way we can.

Remember, it's a relational process more than one-time mission directives. God can speak to us that way, but most of the time He patiently steers us. When our hearts are open to receive and we're willing to trust, even if we mishear one portion of what He's saying, He can adjust us and guide us along the way.

For example, let's say you're considering a job transition. One approach would be to search for the best position with the highest pay, submit your resume and application, and then take the job. If the role is in a different city, you come to your pastor or Small Group leader and ask, "Do you know of a great church in this area?"

At this point, you've significantly limited the involvement of your relationships.

A different approach would be to back up and invite wisdom into the process sooner. This doesn't mean you're asking a pastor or a Small Group leader for permission to change your career path. But you *are* opening yourself up to God's voice and perspective at a deeper level. As you pray and seek God together, they may help you find opportunities you never would have considered or a hesitation that could protect you from a situation that looks too good to be true.

This doesn't mean you won't have challenges and adversity, but this approach allows you to regularly receive guidance and input from God along the way.

When you find a trusted friend who loves you and cares enough about you to prayerfully be honest with you, even when it's not what you were hoping to hear, this is a great gift from God!

 In order to receive this gift, you have to be willing to put yourself out there. Ecclesiastes 7:5 says it's better to listen to the challenging correction (rebuke) of a wise person than to listen to the song of fools!

In our world today, that song is popular and it's playing all around us.

You can apply this wise approach to any of life's decisions, from which college to attend to marriage and dating, from navigating a financial hardship to walking through a health challenge.

God wants us to receive the wisdom and comfort that comes through bearing one another's burdens as we pray and walk together.

Ecclesiastes 7:5

It is better to heed the rebuke of a wise person than to listen to the song of fools.

When you believe God brings people into your life to help you hear and know Him more, you'll be amazed at how He will speak to you through trusted voices.

In 1 Thessalonians 2:13, we see that Paul was grateful for his relationship with the Thessalonians because when he spoke to them, they treated what he said not as his opinion, but as the voice of God.

They didn't blindly follow anything Paul said, but because of his character and the way his words lined up with Scripture, they prayerfully considered his counsel and wisdom as if God told them Himself.

For those willing to listen, God's voice is still speaking through trusted voices today.

1 Thessalonians 2:13

And we also thank God continually because, when you received the word of God, which you heard from us, you accepted it not as a human word, but as it actually is, the word of God, which is indeed at work in you who believe.

GOD SPEAKS THROUGH TRUSTED VOICES, SO WE PRIORITIZE PEOPLE WHO POINT US TO GOD'S WORD AND MINIMIZE VOICES WHO DON'T.

1 THESSALONIANS 2:13 (NIV)

And we also thank
God continually because,
when you received
the word of God, which
you heard from us,
you accepted it not as a
human word, but as
it actually is, the word of
God, which is indeed
at work in you who
believe.

MEMORY VERSE

DISCUSSION QUESTIONS

1. Why is it important to consider the source of the voices we listen to?

2. Read Proverbs 12:15. What does this verse tell you about foolishness?

3. Why do we have a tendency to use confirmation bias to make poor decisions?

4. Have you ever used confirmation bias to make a bad decision in the past? Explain.

5. According to Proverbs 12:15, what is the solution to making poor choices?

6. Whose advice should we listen to? How do you determine if someone is a good person from whom to seek advice? What should be the criteria?

7. Look at the list of five bullet points on page 102. Who in your life fits this list (or comes relatively close)?

8. Is there a decision you are trying to make, or an issue you need wisdom handling? What is it?

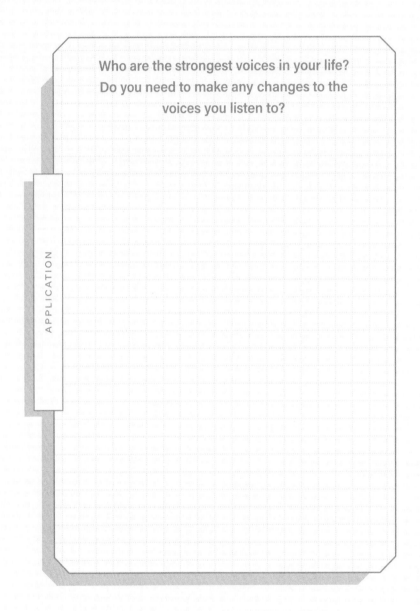

Who are the strongest voices in your life?
Do you need to make any changes to the
voices you listen to?

APPLICATION

WEEK FIVE

GOD SPEAKS THROUGH OUR CONSCIENCE/ INNER WITNESS

CONCEPT

We hear God through His Word. We recognize God's voice by understanding the big principles and patterns of Scripture.

We hear God as the Holy Spirit leads us and guides us into all truth, reminding us of everything Jesus said.

We hear God through trusted voices who love us, encourage us, correct us, offer wisdom, and help us pray through decisions, attitudes, and emotions.

And we hear God through our conscience—our inner witness—the internal sense of right and wrong God gives to every human being.

Have you ever tried to explain your conscience to someone else? On one hand, it's simple: this intuitive feeling that something is either right or wrong, good or bad. Somehow . . . we just know.

On the other hand, it's complicated: we can't prove it, it can surprise us, and we often end up wrestling with it.

Paul mentions the role of the conscience throughout the New Testament.

✳ When he was on trial, he told the religious leaders he fulfilled his duty to God in good conscience and he told the governor he always strived to keep his conscience clear before God and man.

✳ He tells the Romans that sometimes our conscience accuses us and sometimes it defends us. Later, when he's working hard to make a point, he tells them he's not lying because the Holy Spirit confirmed it through his conscience.

✳ But Paul also knew our conscience isn't perfect and it's not our primary standard for hearing God's voice. He tells the Corinthians that even though his conscience was clear, it didn't make him innocent. God's judgment superseded the verdict his conscience provided. Later he tells them some people have a weak conscience so they can easily be defiled by making bad choices. He told Timothy some people damage or sear their conscience through their deception and disobedience.

Acts 23:1

Paul looked straight at the Sanhedrin and said, "My brothers, I have fulfilled my duty to God in all good conscience to this day."

Acts 24:16

So I strive always to keep my conscience clear before God and man.

Romans 2:15

They show that the requirements of the law are written on their hearts, their consciences also bearing witness, and their thoughts sometimes accusing them and at other times even defending them.

Romans 9:1

I speak the truth in Christ—I am not lying, my conscience confirms it through the Holy Spirit.

---

1 Corinthians 4:4

My conscience is clear, but that does not make me innocent. It is the Lord who judges me.

1 Corinthians 8:7

But not everyone possesses this knowledge. Some people are still so accustomed to idols that when they eat sacrificial food they think of it as having been sacrificed to a god, and since their conscience is weak, it is defiled.

1 Timothy 4:2

Such teachings come through hypocritical liars, whose consciences have been seared as with a hot iron.

❋ At the same time, he tells Timothy that people who have a good conscience, a pure heart, and a sincere faith are consistently able to love others well.

Our conscience, our inner witness, is part of the recipe God has given us to hear and know Him, but like everything else, we have to develop it.

In his second letter to the Corinthians, Paul says that he and his ministry partners knew they had served and loved them with integrity and sincerity, not on the basis of worldly wisdom but through the grace of God.

❋ How could they be so confident? Because their conscience testified and confirmed it was true.

Our conscience is like a built-in receiver. It's meant to be tuned to God's frequency with an open channel so we can be ready to hear what God wants to say to us. It's delicate and needs to be cared for because when we're not careful, it can be damaged or misinterpreted.

You might be thinking, *Okay, but how does this work? How will I know?*

---

1 Timothy 1:5

The goal of this command is love, which comes from a pure heart and a good conscience and a sincere faith.

2 Corinthians 1:12

Now this is our boast: Our conscience testifies that we have conducted ourselves in the world, and especially in our relations with you, with integrity and godly sincerity. We have done so, relying not on worldly wisdom but on God's grace.

CONTEXT

✳ Before Jesus ascended into heaven, He told His disciples to wait in the city for the promise of the Father. He explained this promise would be power to be His witness. These followers are gathered together in an upper room in Jerusalem on the day of Pentecost. The Holy Spirit comes on them just like Jesus promised.

✳ This creates a commotion, and the people who have come to celebrate Pentecost want to know what's happening.[1] In response, Peter preaches his first sermon and 3,000 people repent and become followers of Jesus.

In his message, Peter explains what happened through an ancient promise from the book of Joel, written at least 500 years earlier. Joel was a prophet, someone who spoke on behalf of God like Moses and Samuel, and he told the disobedient and unfaithful people of God to return to Him with their hearts. God's desire was to protect and provide for His people, and to repay them for the years their enemies had stolen.

Acts 1:8

"But you will receive power when the Holy Spirit comes on you; and you will be my witnesses in Jerusalem, and in all Judea and Samaria, and to the ends of the earth."

Acts 2:41

Those who accepted his message were baptized, and about three thousand were added to their number that day.

---

1 Pentecost comes from the Greek word "50," because it was traditionally celebrated 50 days after Passover. After Jesus' death and resurrection (which happened during and as the fulfillment of Passover), followers of Christ celebrated Pentecost 50 days after Easter Sunday.

One of the primary ways they would know this was happening was that God's Spirit would be poured out on all people. Not just priests, prophets, and kings, but the everyday person would hear God.

Peter basically tells the people that because of Jesus, the long-awaited Day of the Lord has come. No more waiting. It's happening right now, in real time, right in front of you.

Notice what happens when God pours His Spirit on all people: they experience and receive it in different ways, but each expression is a way God speaks His Word and His heart to them. It could be a prophetic word of encouragement spoken through someone else. It could be a dream. It could be a vision.

We are not meant to be distracted by how. In fact, Scripture wants us to see that all of these are ways God speaks to us, and which way He chooses depends on our personalities and the way He has wired us.

When the Bible talks about the Day of the Lord, it's not talking about a particular day on the calendar. It means we've entered a new era in our relationship, where God has made Himself present among the people in a powerful way.

And in case it's not clear when the Bible says "all people" in verse 28, God lets us know He means sons and daughters, old and young men, servants, men and women . . . all of us!

. . . your old men will dream dreams

JOEL 2:28-29 (NIV)

[28] "And afterward,
I will pour out
my Spirit on all people.
Your sons and daughters
will prophesy,
your old men
will dream dreams,
your young men
will see visions.
[29] Even on my servants,
both men and women,
I will pour out my
Spirit in those days."

. . . your young men will see visions.

CAUTION

Remember, we learn to hear and trust God's voice through His Word. **Get ready—this is an area where this WILL be tested!**

No voice is more compelling or capable of deceiving us than our own internal monologue. Thoughts lead to feelings, feelings lead to desires, and once we really want something, our heart enlists our head to justify why it's the right thing to do.

Follow your heart, live your truth, and be yourself are the most viral and trusted cultural messages we hear. All three of these feelings are in direct contradiction to what God says in His Word.

Many people think, *Why would God give me these desires if He didn't want me to act on them?* There are several problems with this. Not every desire you have comes from God. Jeremiah 17:9 says that the heart is the most deceitful of all things, and desperately wicked. This is why Proverbs 4:23 (NLT) reminds us: "Guard your heart above all else, for it determines the course of your life."

How do you know if you're guarding your heart? Whenever there's a conflict between your feelings and God's Word, you submit to His Word.

WHAT DOES THIS MEAN FOR US?

On the Day of the Lord, God promised to pour out His Spirit on all people. Peter said that in Jesus, this day has come.

We're living it now. We can expect God to speak to us. We can ask for dreams, visions, and encouraging words (that's what *prophecy* means).

God has given us a built-in receiver, a conscience, an internal way of knowing right and wrong. This conscience gets stronger when it's combined with a pure heart, sincere faith, and genuine love.

So how does our conscience/inner witness help us interpret the Spirit, poured out on all people?

First, because your conscience is part of you, it's going to sound like you. Not the selfish, frustrated, overly emotional version of you. The best version of you. The you that's only possible when it's combined with the goodness and grace of God.

Second, because it's part of you, it's going to work through your personality. Some people get a directional word from their conscience. Others may see a picture that helps them think about it from a different perspective. Some people's imaginations create a movie in their mind as if they can see what will happen if they follow or ignore their conscience. Other people simply know what they're supposed to do through a strong feeling.

As you strengthen and develop your conscience over the years, you will likely experience all of these, but many people develop a pattern they can depend on.

Finally, when the Bible talks about issues of conscience, it's not talking about areas where there are clear standards. "Should I stay faithful to my spouse?" is not an issue of conscience.

Ephesians 5 compares the love between a husband and a wife to the love between Jesus and His Church. Verse 25 tells husbands to love their wives like Christ loved the Church and gave Himself up for her, and verse 33b says wives must respect their husbands. That's the standard.

Typically, when God speaks through our conscience, He doesn't shout or dictate our response. Instead, He softly tells us, "Ask your friend about their marriage . . . pray for them and encourage them." Or He brings a specific person to mind who may have offended you: "Text them and tell them you've been thinking about them and how much you love and appreciate them."

You may think, *That's silly. That's not God. I'm just imagining it.*

He may say, "Have you thought about spending less time watching that show or scrolling through your social media? It makes you frustrated, worried, and angry." You can dismiss it as nothing . . . or you can ask God if He's speaking to you.

There's no formula. It's a relationship. He won't force you, but He will invite you. You may be thinking, *Where do I even start?* Great question. Just be open and ready.

Strengthening our conscience is more about inviting God to speak to everyday areas of our lives, not in a "super-spiritual" or overly religious way but giving Him the opportunity to influence and guide us in our hobbies, our work life, our errands, and in all the countless moments we experience over the course of the day.

When we invite Him to speak to us in these moments, we're often surprised to see how regularly He shows up. And like anything in life, there's a little bit of a learning curve. It takes faith to believe and trust it's Him.

Because He's a loving Father, He'll never scold us for inviting Him to speak to us about the things we care about. And when He speaks, we show our love and gratitude by being careful not to harden our hearts and to respond to what He says.

The good news is, even when we miss His subtle cues or misunderstand the message, when we decide we're going to do our best to listen, He patiently meets us and guides us back on the path.

WHAT DO I DO WITH THIS?

Like most communication devices, our conscience/inner witness has at least two channels: incoming and outgoing. Both need to be cultivated and developed. Most people find one approach easier than the other.

OUTGOING	INCOMING

When you're wrestling with a decision, prayer request, or challenging situation, do you pray and ask God to speak to you?

When you're reading your Bible, listening to a message, praying, or in worship, and you know God's speaking to you and asking you to obey, is it hard for you to respond?

Here are some practical things you can do to grow:

- Write down your need and put it in a place where you'll see it each day.
- Search the Word to see where it speaks to what you're facing.
- Talk about the issue with God. Tell Him what you're feeling. Ask Him to help you.
- Tell two or three trusted voices what you're facing and ask them to pray with you and for you.

Here are some practical things you can do to grow:

- Write down what He spoke to you and put it in a place where you'll see it.
- Ask Him to show you practically how to live this way.
- Write down two or three obstacles that make this change difficult.
- Tell two or three trusted voices what God spoke to you. Ask them to help you live it out.

GOD SPEAKS THROUGH OUR CONSCIENCE/ INNER WITNESS, SO WE MUST OVERCOME OUR FEELINGS AND EMOTIONS IN ORDER TO SUBMIT TO GOD'S WORD.

JEREMIAH 33:3 (NIV)

"Call to me and
I will answer you and
tell you great and
unsearchable things
you do not know."

1. How would you describe the voice of your conscience?

2. Is our conscience always right? How do we know when we can trust it?

3. The Bible teaches that your conscience can become "seared" through deception and disobedience (1 Timothy 4:2). What do you think it means to have a seared conscience? How would that affect someone?

4. In what ways can you help your conscience become more sensitive to God's voice?

5. Page 123 talks about how your conscience is a part of your personality. This can affect how you sense God speaking to you. For example:

"Some people get a directional word from their conscience. Others may see a picture that helps them think about it from a different perspective. Some people's imaginations create a movie in their mind as if they can see what will happen if they follow or ignore their conscience. Other people simply know what they're supposed to do through a strong feeling."

Have you ever felt God speak to you in one of these ways? Does God speak to you more often in one particular way than the others?

6. We need to develop both our incoming and outgoing channels of communication with God. How would you describe the difference between those two channels?

7. Do you struggle more with the incoming channel or the outgoing? Explain.

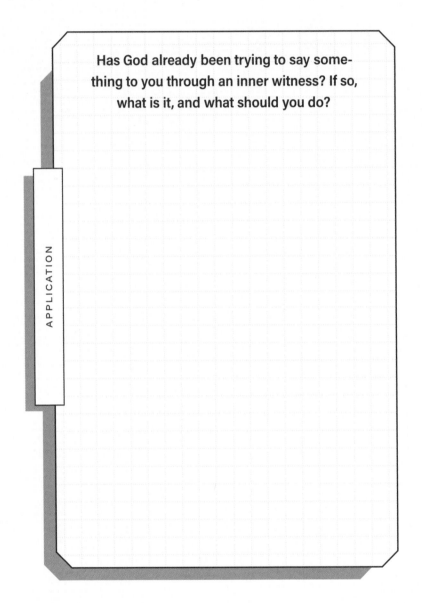

APPLICATION

Has God already been trying to say something to you through an inner witness? If so, what is it, and what should you do?

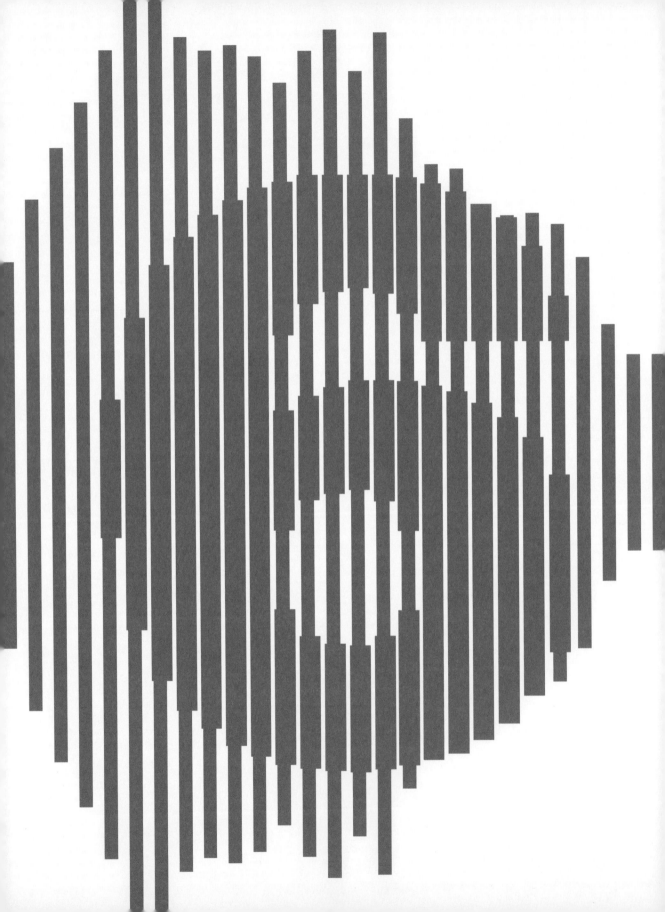

GOD SPEAKS THROUGH EVENTS IN OUR LIVES

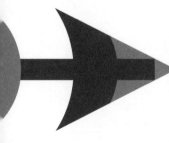 # CONCEPT

No organ in our body uses as much energy as our brains. Because they're high functioning, they're constantly looking for ways to conserve energy. One of the easiest ways for our brains to conserve energy is to make things simple.

We think, *Just tell me what to do*, or *Get to the point*. You may be thinking that right now.

But many of the important things in life are not simple. They're nuanced. They require balancing two things that are true at the same time.

The last category of how God speaks to us is one of those complicated, nuanced truths. It's also important.

Here's the first part: God can, and does, speak to us through our circumstances, or the events of our lives.

Here's the second part: Not everything that happens to us in our lives is God speaking to us, and if we relate to Him this way, it's going to be hard on us.

You can probably relate to both of these ideas. Something happens and you wonder, *Is that God? Is He punishing me? Is He blessing me? What's He trying to say?*

This is normal. One extreme is to think, *That's dumb. God doesn't have anything to do with it.* The other extreme would be to always attribute every moment as some sort of secret message from God.

Neither of these approaches are helpful. Which leaves us back at square one. How do we move forward? Our goal is to live in the tension. We consider both things at the same time while leaning into the trust we have in our relationship with God.

Let's do a quick review.

We know God is a communicator—it's His nature that He wants us to know and hear His voice.

We also know it can be difficult for us to hear Him for a number of reasons: His voice can be drowned out by other voices, we don't recognize His voice, there's an enemy running interference, we think He doesn't see us and doesn't care, we're selfish and have our own agendas, etc.

Many Bible scholars believe Job is likely the oldest book in the Bible. You could summarize the entire story as one man's attempt to discern what God was saying to him through the events of his life.

Job 33:14 (NLT) confirms our challenge: "'For God speaks again and again, though people do not recognize it.'"

What is He trying to say?

In order to better understand this, let's go back to the Word. There is a clear and undeniable pattern of God speaking through the events of our lives.

We don't build a theology (a system of relating to God) based on what He did with one person at one time. But we also don't want to overlook the fact that God has always interacted with people in and through the everyday moments of their lives.

BIBLE PATTERN:
God Speaks through Life Events

When God speaks to Noah, He tells him to build a boat because the world would flood. No human being had ever seen rain. Once the rain came for 40 days and 40 nights, Noah probably felt much more confident that it was God who was speaking to him.[1]

---

1   You can find this part of Noah's story in Genesis 6-7.

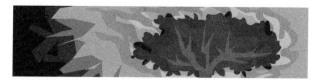

Moses is tending sheep in the wilderness when he spots a bush that's on fire, but the flames aren't destroying it. Moses finds it strange, so he goes over to get a closer look. It's one of the key moments in Scripture. God speaks through the bush, changing not only the lives of Moses and all of the Israelities held captive in Egypt but ultimately the history of the world.[2]

Balaam was what is often called a fortune teller or a witch doctor in certain cultures. He would bless and curse people, so the king of Moab tried to hire him to curse God's people. Balaam was resistant but the king kept insisting. When Balaam gets on his donkey to go see the king, the donkey sees the angel of the Lord, freaks out, and hides.

In his frustration, Balaam beats the donkey . . . and then the story gets crazy. God gives the donkey the ability to speak and he basically says, "What's your deal, bro? Why are you beating me? I've always been good to you." Balaam's eyes are opened, he sees the angel of the Lord and he repents.[3]

---

2 This interesting episode in Moses' life comes from Exodus 3.

3 This fascinating story can be found in Numbers 22.

When God comes to Gideon, he's hiding and afraid. Once God speaks to him and tells him to deliver His people from their enemies with his "mighty strength," Gideon asks for multiple signs in order to know it's really God. He interprets a meal burning up and the presence or absence of dew on a fleece as confirmation it's really God.[4]

God then tells Gideon he has too many soldiers and the way he would get rid of the excess was to watch how they drank water from a river.[5]

After David becomes the king, the Philistines hear about it and come to attack. David asks the Lord if he should meet them in battle. God speaks to David and helps him. The next time they come, David asks again, and this time the Lord tells him to wait until they can hear the sounds of the enemy marching in the tops of the poplar trees.[6]

---

4 This part of Gideon's story can be found in Judges 6.

5 This detail comes from Judges 7:1-7.

6 You can see for yourself in 1 Chronicles 14:8-16.

Elijah's deepest depression comes after his greatest victory. He defeats the prophets of Baal but the wicked queen Jezebel tries to kill him. He takes off and hides in a cave and has an emotional breakdown. God tells Elijah He's going to pass by, and then a mighty wind, an earthquake, and a great fire pass by Elijah. God is not in any of them.

But then Elijah unmistakably hears God's voice in a gentle whisper.[7]

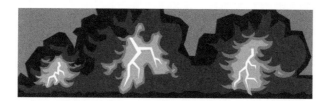

God calls Jonah to Nineveh, but he runs the other way, gets on a boat, and tries to flee. When the boat hits a storm, Jonah knows God is telling him to turn around.[8]

This is not an exhaustive list and you probably noticed all of these moments come from the Old Testament. We could easily trace through similar moments in the New Testament and will look at several in the next section. The point is, we can clearly see a pattern of how God speaks both in and through the events happening in our lives.

---

7 The showdown on Mount Carmel is the second half of 1 Kings 18, but this outstanding window into how God speaks comes from 1 Kings 19:1-18.

8 See Jonah 1.

CONTEXT

We looked at how God poured out His Spirit on the people in **Acts 2** on the day of Pentecost. Peter preaches the first sermon and 3,000 people are added to the Church. They continue to tell people about Jesus and by the beginning of **Acts 4**, there are 5,000 men, not counting women and children, who are now following Jesus as Lord.

The entire adventure of the early Church was the story of God speaking and moving through the events of their daily lives.

In Acts 5, the disciples experience persecution and suffering, which causes them to spread throughout the region.

In Acts 6, they're led by the Spirit to restructure so they can focus on the right roles and be more effective.

In Acts 8, the Spirit sends Philip to Samaria first and then to an Ethiopian.

In Acts 10, God appears to a devout centurion named Cornelius and tells him to send for Peter. Peter didn't think reaching Gentiles was part of the plan so God had to appear to him too and convince him to go. His experience with Cornelius is so significant that it changes the way Peter and the rest of the disciples think about their mission.

In Acts 11, Barnabas goes and gets Saul, the man behind much of the Church's most violent persecution who had a radical encounter with Jesus on the road to Damascus. They spend a year together, meeting with people and teaching in the churches.

We could continue to point out the pattern through each of the chapters, but hopefully, at this point, you recognize what's happening.

This is not to suggest our daily lives are equivalent to how God records the supernatural expansion of His Church in the book of Acts, but His nature doesn't change. The same God who spoke to them through their circumstances is active and present in our lives. We're His sheep—He promised we can recognize His voice too.

This little passage **in Acts 16** encapsulates the approach of believers in the early Church. It's not an exact science. We can't eliminate challenges. Not everything in life is supposed to go smoothly. We grow and learn from God as He meets us in it.

By this point, Saul's name has been changed to Paul and he is one of the most significant and trusted leaders in the Church. His primary mission is to the Gentiles, people who were not Israelites by natural birth.

ACTS 16:6-10 (NIV)

⁶ Paul and his companions traveled throughout the region of Phrygia and Galatia, having been kept by the Holy Spirit from preaching the word in the province of Asia. ⁷ When they came to the border of Mysia, they tried to enter Bithynia, but the Spirit of Jesus would not allow them to. ⁸ So they passed by Mysia and went down to Troas. ⁹ During the night Paul had a vision of a man of Macedonia standing and begging him, "Come over to Macedonia and help us." ¹⁰ After Paul had seen the vision, we got ready at once to leave for Macedonia, concluding that God had called us to preach the gospel to them.

CAUTION

One more time . . . we learn to hear and trust God's voice through His Word. Hearing God speak through events in our lives may be the most difficult way to hear Him in the moment. More commonly, we recognize this one when we look back later.

At times throughout their lives, every Christ-follower will wonder, *What are you doing, Lord? Did you forget about me? What am I supposed to do?*

This puts us in a delicate place. Often, we're tempted to make drastic or reactionary decisions. It's never wise to make major life moves when we're emotional. God doesn't force us or hammer us; He works with us through faith and patience.

And yet, God will speak to us through the events in our lives. He wants to build our faith. He wants us to grow in our love and generosity toward others. He wants to expand our confidence in what He's able to do.

This always works in conjunction with His Word, the Holy Spirit, and trusted voices. If you feel like you're hearing God say, "You better do this now, or you'll never get another chance!" It's not God because the Word says He's good, ready to forgive, and abounding in love to all who call on Him in Psalm 86:5.

His grace and His love don't run out. He's not looking for ways to give us less or be less involved in our lives. He's present and ready to speak to those who will listen.

WHAT DOES THIS MEAN FOR US?

Notice the language the Bible uses in Acts 16:

"... kept by the Holy Spirit from preaching the word in the province of Asia."

"... they tried to enter Bithynia, but the Spirit of Jesus would not allow them to."

"During the night Paul had a vision of a man of Macedonia ..."

"... we got ready at once to leave for Macedonia, concluding that God had called us ..."

In different ways, for different reasons, God is leading and guiding them through the events of their daily lives.

You're probably thinking, *Well, that's Paul building the early church. That's a long way from my life. Is God really involved in my life?*

Remember, God's character doesn't change. And our primary goal is not to crack the code or to discover a secret formula for life. The goal is to know and love Him more, to hear His voice, and to obey.

We want to be open and aware whenever God wants to speak to us about any part of our lives.

We're not trying to decode the deeper meaning of every life event, but we can't deny there is a clear pattern in Scripture. Most of the time, you can't see it when you're in it, only later.

The goal is not to beat yourself up for not listening or making the right choices. Just as He did in the book of Acts, God gently and lovingly corrects those who put their trust in Him.

We tend to get frustrated when things don't go the way we want them to, when certain doors close, when our timelines and plans get thrown out. There's nothing wrong with making plans, having goals, and building timelines.

But we don't make them more important than God.

The pattern of Scripture, from the Old Testament to the New Testament, shows us many times that when we think God is silent or disinterested, He's working for our good behind the scenes in ways we don't understand.

He doesn't ask us to mastermind the outcomes of our lives. What He asks is for us to be ready to listen, to trust Him, and when we hear His voice, to obey.

WHAT DO I DO WITH THIS?

In light of this pattern, there are three simple applications every follower of Christ can make on a regular basis.

First, simply ask God in prayer, "Lord, are You speaking to me through this circumstance? I'm listening and open to anything You want to say."

Second, when He responds in any of the ways we've learned about (through His Word, through the Holy Spirit, through trusted voices, through your conscience/inner witness), do what He asks you to do.

Third, whenever you're in a significant life event or circumstance, reflect on His goodness and faithfulness in the past. Over and over throughout His Word, God tells His people to "remember." It builds our faith and brings us closer to Him.

GOD
SPEAKS
THROUGH
EVENTS IN
OUR LIVES,
SO WE NEED TO
BE OPEN TO WHAT
HE IS SAYING
AT ANY TIME
WHILE
REMEMBERING
HIS WORD,
THE HOLY SPIRIT,
AND TRUSTED
VOICES NEED TO
CONFIRM IT.

PSALM 85:8 (NLT)

I listen carefully to what God the Lord is saying, for he speaks peace to his faithful people. But let them not return to their foolish ways.

1. There are two extremes regarding how we view circumstances. One extreme is to think God doesn't use circumstances to speak to us at all, and the other extreme is to think that every circumstance is a message from God. Do you tend to lean one way or the other? Explain.

2. Read Acts 16:6-10. According to these verses, how was God working through Paul's circumstances?

3. Why would God use circumstances to try to get our attention?

4. Do you think God still uses circumstances today to speak to us? Explain.

5. Have you ever felt like God was using a certain situation to get your attention or to tell you something? What was it?

6. How can we know if God is trying to speak to us through a particular circumstance?

7. Whenever you find yourself in a significant life event or circumstance, why is it helpful to reflect on God's goodness and faithfulness in the past?

8. Looking at all the ways God speaks to us—through His Word, through the Holy Spirit, through trusted voices, through our conscience, and through circumstances—which is the most important? Why?

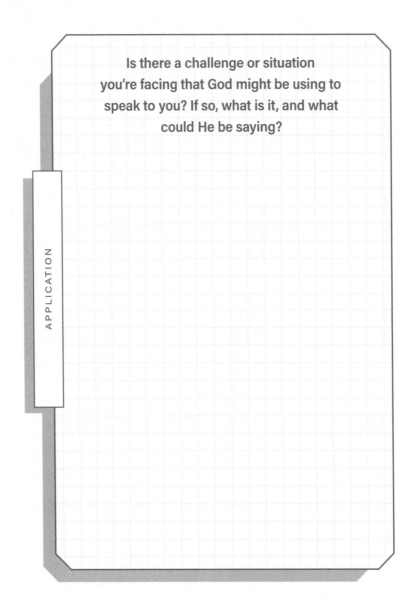

Is there a challenge or situation
you're facing that God might be using to
speak to you? If so, what is it, and what
could He be saying?

APPLICATION

TO CONCLUDE OUR STUDY TOGETHER,

we aren't trying to oversimplify a complex topic. However, we want to be clear that hearing God hinges on these three important truths:

1.
The Bible (God's Word) is our primary
source to hear from God. It's authoritative
and everything else submits to it.

2.
The Holy Spirit agrees with God's Word
and always points us back to what Jesus said.

3.
You want to find trusted voices that
point you back to God's Word and the Holy Spirit
and are in agreement with them.

FOR MORE RESOURCES, VISIT US ONLINE!

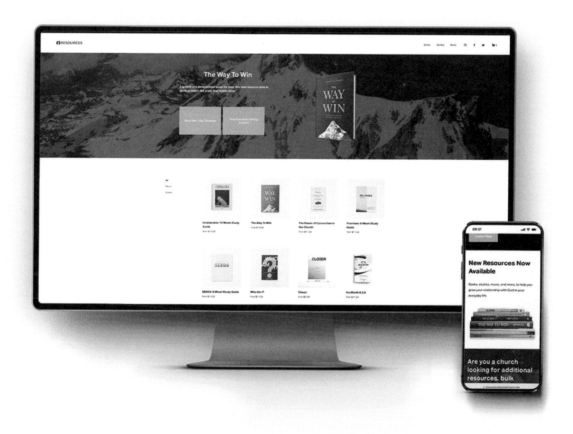

KEY TRUTHS AND SCRIPTURE CARDS

These key truths and Scripture memory cards correspond to each week in the *Hearing God* study.

We encourage you to think about these key truths and memorize these verses each week of *Hearing God.* To help, detach these cards and put them somewhere visible, like the dash of your car, the back of your phone, your desk at work, or your bathroom mirror.

1 THESSALONIANS 2:13

And we also th
God continually b
when you recei
word of God, w
heard from us, yo
it not as a human
it actually is
of God, which
at work in yo

We
God S
Tr

JOHN 10:27 (NIV)

"My sheep listen
to my voice;
I know them, and
they follow me."

2 TIMOTHY 3:16 (NIV)

All Scripture is
God-breathed and
is useful for
teaching, rebuking,
correcting and

KEY TRUTHS TO HEARING GOD

INTRODUCTION:
God speaks, so we need to listen.

WEEK 1:
God speaks through His Word, so we regularly read the Bible.

WEEK 2:
God speaks through patterns and principles in His Word, so we take steps to keep growing in our understanding of Scripture.

WEEK 3:
God speaks through the Holy Spirit, so we can remember what Jesus said and be guided into all truth.

WEEK 4:
God speaks through trusted voices, so we prioritize people who point us to God's Word and minimize voices who don't.

WEEK 5:
God speaks through our conscience/inner witness, so we must overcome our feelings and emotions in order to submit to God's Word.

WEEK 6:
God speaks through events in our lives, so we need to be open to what He is saying at any time while remembering His Word, the Holy Spirit, and trusted voices need to confirm it.

RECOGNIZING HIS VOICE
IN A WORLD FULL OF NOISE

HEARING
GOD

JOHN 10:27 (NIV)

"My sheep listen
to my voice;
I know them, and
they follow me."

Introduction
God Speaks—He's a
Communicator

1 SAMUEL 3:10 (NIV)

The Lord came and
stood there, calling as
at the other times,
"Samuel! Samuel!"

Then Samuel said,
"Speak, for your servant
is listening."

Week One
God Speaks
through His Word

2 TIMOTHY 3:16 (NIV)

All Scripture is
God-breathed and
is useful for
teaching, rebuking,
correcting and training
in righteousness.

Week Two
God Speaks through Patterns
& Principles in His Word

JOHN 14:26 (NIV)

"But the Advocate,
the Holy Spirit,
whom the Father
will send in my name,
will teach you
all things and will
remind you of everything
I have said to you."

Week Three
God Speaks through
the Holy Spirit

1 THESSALONIANS 2:13 (NIV)

And we also thank
God continually because,
when you received the
word of God, which you
heard from us, you accepted
it not as a human word, but as
it actually is, the word
of God, which is indeed
at work in you who believe.

Week Four
God Speaks through
Trusted Voices

JEREMIAH 33:3 (NIV)

"Call to me and
I will answer you and
tell you great and
unsearchable things
you do not know."

Week Five
God Speaks through our
Conscience/Inner Witness

PSALM 85:8 (NLT)

I listen carefully to
what God the
Lord is saying, for he
speaks peace to
his faithful people.
But let them not
return to their foolish
ways.

Week Six
God Speaks through
Events in Our Lives

HEARING
GOD

HEARING
GOD

HEARING
GOD

HEARING
GOD

HEARING
GOD

HEARING
GOD

HEARING
GOD